Paint the Next Sunrise

A FUTURE FOR HUNTING AND FISHING

for Doug ("Spongee")

BY MARK STRAND

Mark Strand

here's to a bright future for our outdoor traditions — thanks for your support!

BEAVER'S POND
PRESS

ISBN 10: 1-59298-296-4

ISBN 13: 978-1-59298-296-7

Library of Congress Catalog Number: 2009931548

Printed in the United States of America
First Printing: 2009

13   12   11   10   09   5   4   3   2   1

Cover and interior design by Monette Kollodge
All photos by the author, by his father Dick Strand, and by Jill, Willie or Samantha

BEAVER'S POND
PRESS

Beaver's Pond Press, Inc.
7104 Ohms Lane, Suite 101
Edina, MN 55439-2129
(952) 829-8818
www.BeaversPondPress.com

To order, visit www.BookHouseFulfillment.com or call 1-800-901-3480.
Reseller discounts available.

Dedication

For Dad, who did a great job within the old system, of bringing my mom and all five kids into the traditional outdoor sports.

For his uncle Sid, who did the same thing for my Dad and my uncle, Roger.

For uncle Roger, who devotes his life to conservation and helping people experience the wonders of hunting and fishing.

For all beginners who will use the new system to find fun and satisfaction for the same reasons we did.

Foreword

If we know what's good for us, we don't hesitate when offered organic versus synthetic when it comes to clothes or food.

Going "green" whenever practical is a quick "yes" in most people's books as well.

But what about our heads? They're buried in the seemingly limitless virtual world offered by TV, DVD, and the Internet. In high definition, no less.

We've got great sports and teams to root for, but by their design these sports are synthetic in the sense they were "invented" by someone, more or less out of thin air, involving balls, rules, quorums, time, scores.

Whether we realize it or not, we all have a deep longing for an organic connection with the natural world. It just might be the most important missing component in most people's lives.

Going to a place where semblance of a "natural world" can be found, and getting to know how, when, and where the things that live there are connected, can provide a spiritual and intellectual satisfaction that defines the experience and provides a link in the chain to understanding ourselves and our place in the world.

It's also the best way to get to really know the creatures–whether they be bugs, bears, butterflies, or bass.

Fishing does it for me. Of course, there are other ways as well. Please read this book, because it offers an irresistible proposition.

– Larry Dahlberg, Hall of Fame fisherman and host of
'The Hunt for Big Fish' TV show

Chapter One:
Old System, New Challenges

A little thumb pushed down on the button of a youth rod-and-reel combo, the rod whipped back and forth, and a rubber frog with a weedless hook in it sailed across the sky and landed on the water. It came down a long way from the original aiming point, but close enough for this operation, because as long as your hook is in the water there's a chance.

It was getting close to sunset. The water was a blend of gun barrel blue and shades of gray across a bay also dotted with dark green lily pads. The fake frog was splashing across the surface and then a bass changed everything when it tried to eat the frog.

On the cover of outdoor magazines of that time (early 1960s) it would have been easy to find a painting of this very picture, water everywhere out at the end of the line, a big bass thrashing, anglers in an old boat, oars in the water. The frog was mine, and the weight of the frantic bass in my hands, cranking with every bit of power on that old hinge-reel combo from South Bend. The fish was using my line to cut underwater weeds, and I was making every mistake in the book. My dad was telling me not to horse him. I had no idea what that meant, instructions from a lesson not yet learned, and then the fish jumped and got off.

After it was over, I sat there and cried, ankles bent on the curved aluminum floor of the old boat, high-top tennis shoes rocking on rivets, tears soaking into an overstuffed orange life jacket that you remember if you grew up in those days. The life jacket was a real pain in the butt, like an airbag that went off around your neck, but you were expected to keep it on, no matter how tightly your dad cinched it up, and make a cast into that little opening he was pointing to with one of the oars.

Dad tried to get me to keep fishing, but there was nothing to fish for.

At least, that's the way it felt at the time. When a big fish gets off, it's deflating for anybody. When your first decent fish gets off, it can be devastating for a beginner.

In reality, there had been a transfer of passion during the brief battle with that fish. But how could a little kid know anything about that?

Now, I understand why Dad tied a 'rubber frog' to the end of my line. That's what he called them, right up to the end. (He also persisted in calling plastic worms rubber worms, even after hip young anglers, including myself, tried to teach him the 'correct' new term.) It was actually a Bill's Bass Frog. I remember that, because we talked about it many times. Brilliant move on Dad's part, because the bait floated and was almost completely weedless. Even a little kid had a hard time getting into trouble with a Bill's Bass Frog. I still have some of them in my tackle box, the same ones passed down from my dad's tackle box. As I got older and knew everything about how to optimize 'rubber' frogs for hooking percentage, I cut out the original hook and weed guard and tried my own inventions, some of which might have improved hooking percentage a little.

My kids have fished with those same frogs.

Back to the bass that got away. We were operating out of a small boat that also held at least one of my brothers or sisters (I honestly can't remember for sure), and we were firing away. We knew that we were trying to get a fish to bite, but had no idea where the next cast was going to end up. There was a real possibility it could sail deep onto dry land, or high in a tree. If it landed on shore, it was usually no biggie, because one of us could trace the line and free the hook without major problems. But I can still remember how quiet we were whenever a lure got stuck high in a tree. One of us held the front of the boat against shore, and Dad knocked branches into the water (and the boat) with an outstretched oar, trying to get the lure out of the sky. Because of the great tension during times like that, and because it was often my lure stuck in an overhead branch, the sound of aluminum scraping against shoreline brush, to this day, is harder for me to listen to than fingernails on a chalkboard.

If my dad had been out there by himself on that same evening, he would have boated dozens of nice bass. Instead he was passing it on, using the old system, teaching his own kids how to fish. The battle with that bass took place on a little lake in northern Minnesota, but it could happen today on plenty of other lakes, anywhere. It wasn't a dream, fly-in destination. It was just a lake close to a campground where my parents pitched a tent and took us fishing.

In the many years since that evening, many things have changed. Divorce rates have made it increasingly common for any given kid to grow up in a single-parent household. More people are crowded onto the same finite amount of land. We are an increasingly urbanized, technology driven, extremely busy human race, with apparently less time and inclination to go fishing or hunting. For these reasons and more, the chances are now slimmer that this kind of scene would play itself out, featuring a father and his own kids. But what are we supposed to do about that? Those of us who still fish because we love it could sit there in our modern boats, both feet flat on the carpeted floor, and shed grown-up tears about how things aren't like they used to be.

Those of us who should be keepers of the flame all have our own stories, and most of them were written during a time when young boys (and less commonly, girls) were handed the tradition of fishing and hunting by their own fathers or grandfathers. I have other stories involving my dad and BB guns and .22 rifles and learning to recognize what a dog looks like when it gets birdy, but the real news of the day is this: that train has left the station. Nowadays, many of us sit on a bench at that vacant station wishing for the days when 'a guy' could take his kid over by the edge of the field and teach him how to shoot, and there might even be a rabbit the kid could aim at rather than a soda can. Pining for things that once were is a proven recipe for nostalgia, but conspires against finding creative solutions that match the way things are now.

According to people who count this kind of stuff, participation in traditional outdoor sports among Americans is declining. Direct and accurate comparisons, however, of older participation studies with recent ones is considered impossible, due to significant changes in polling methods.

Since 1955, the U.S. Department of the Interior, Fish and Wildlife Service and the U.S. Department of Commerce, Bureau of the Census, have been tracking "Fishing, Hunting and Wildlife-

Associated Recreation," as the studies are called. More recently, Outdoor Industry Foundation has been collecting detailed participation data that should help track trends more accurately in the future (but hunting was only added to these surveys in 2005).

Best attempts at comparing data from early surveys would suggest that hunting participation has been on a steady decline since about the mid-1970s. The numbers in some ways appear to be more favorable with respect to fishing, but recent annual polls reveal a downward trend in angler numbers, too. Just comparing fishing participation from 2004 to 2005, the number of anglers in America dropped by 3.1 million.

A 1991-2001 study done by the U.S. Fish and Wildlife Service showed that the national participation rate in hunting among people 16-24 years old dropped 31 percent. Fishing participation declined 32 percent, just in that time span alone. Similar numbers are seen in other age groups, strong evidence of a bleak future for these sports unless something significant changes.

"It's clear," says Tim Kelly, a researcher for the Minnesota Department of Natural Resources, "that fewer young people are getting involved in fishing and young adults are dropping out." In Minnesota, the situation is viewed as a threat to businesses that rely on fishing and hunting participation, so the state is trying to come up with a recruitment campaign. So far, ideas include billboards and more money for fishing clinics aimed at young people. As is common, the 'ongoing' part of the equation is not addressed.

Another notable finding is that, even among those who continue to participate, frequency of outings is declining. From the most recent Outdoor Industry Foundation study, average number of outings for anglers dropped from 18 to 14 between 2004 and 2005. "To increase participation," OIF says in its executive summary, "new twists on old activities are needed that make the activity more appealing."

Rather than relying on numbers, common sense usually provides clear glimpses at the interplay of dynamics. In the 'glory days' of hunting and fishing in America–back when participation rates were not a concern–there were fewer people living in the same amount of space. It was easier for hunters to knock on the door of a farmer and get permission to go hunting, and it was easier to find a suitable place, where it was legal, to practice shooting, either for its own sake or as warmup for hunting season. It seemed like there was more room out there on the water, too. (This might be due, in part, to modern boats that let us zip from one end of the lake to the other in a few minutes, and GPS units that lead us from one high-percentage spot to the next.)

Add more people to a finite amount of land (exactly what we are doing, by the hour) and it gets more difficult to deliver quality hunting and fishing experiences.

So what does common sense tell us about the true picture and prospects for a bright future?

Sheer numbers of us on the landscape are not likely to go down unless something catastrophic occurs. Despite statistics that show declining rates of participation, it can appear to be curiously congested at good hunting and fishing spots. These sports, because they are defined by pursuit and capture of wild animals in natural settings, rely upon natural settings that are at least relatively uncrowded.

We have a broken down old mentoring system, beginners who need help learning the basics, and challenges finding places for all of us to fish and hunt.

How are we going to find answers, when there is so much to be depressed about?

We can do it, by coming to terms with today's world, by concentrating on the issue of access, and perhaps by redefining the experience, especially when it comes to hunting.

In the summary of virtually every study documenting declining participation rates, you will find a list of rhetorical questions wondering "what can be done?" to slow or reverse the decline. The fatal flaw in most of what is currently being tried (no fault of the people and organizations putting forth honest energy and effort) is that almost all initiatives center around once-a-year, or once-a-lifetime, events. Most beginners are anonymous, because we don't stay with them, help them, answer their questions, or even take them again. Clinics under big tents, where kids cast at targets on the grass and learn to tie knots, do not pair kids up with the wonders of fishing.

When it comes to hunting, we see true grasping at straws, including lowering the age at which kids can shoot the gun on a hunting trip. The logic is that if we wait until they're 12 years old to put them on the firing line, we have probably lost them to other hobbies.

In the real world, we cannot wish things away, including the fact that video games, organized sports, the Internet, and more compete for the attention of young people. Even in simpler times, other interests competed for the attention of young people. Blood relatives who volunteered to mentor used to be in greater supply, too.

But there's more reason for optimism than you might think. If we keep our eyes wide open, identify real needs at the core, and create a new system for finding, inspiring, and helping newcomers, a new way can create a new day.

Chapter Two:
Paint the Next Sunrise

Huge challenges demand creative solutions and never-say-die dedication to them. That's what it will take to create a bright future for the traditional outdoor sports. Even though the old guard (I'm part of it) has been slow to react to evolving realities, rather than panic we should come to terms with inevitability of change. Everything changes.

Let's get a grip on human nature, right out of the blocks. Let's market hunting and fishing to potential newcomers in a way that lights the pilot light on what can be a latent desire to connect with real wild places and real wild creatures. Even in the Wild West days, some hunters probably didn't love sneaking through muddy marshes to waylay a critter for that night's supper. If given the choice, they might have ordered a pizza and put their feet up by the fire.

Today's world is full of people who have never tried fishing or hunting. That doesn't mean they are permanently disinterested. It does mean we have to get them to look up from their gaming systems and climate-controlled surroundings and get them to come outside, where they can discover that the real thing is even more amazing than high resolution graphics. We have to do a lot of things differently than we used to, in many cases defining 'wild' as a small woodlot or little lake adjacent to urban centers. Kids do not come out of the womb seeking video games or french fries; they discover what they like after being sent inspiring invitations and trying the free samples.

We have the best of all leisure time activities to offer, but we stink at enticement and training. Many times, the hunting and fishing industry is so preoccupied with trying to impress and win over the small percentage of already hardcore participants that it succeeds mainly in making these sports seem complicated, expensive, competitive and exclusive. When that's the message, who, among potential newcomers, would feel welcome– or optimistic about success– unless they'd grown up in a swamp with a knife in their teeth and the ability to call animals with their voice?

The smoke signals we send out to potential newcomers should be simpler, more inspirational, more full of the real message: that it's possible to find success right away in hunting and fishing, and that these sports are a lot of fun. Beginners don't have to start at the top, and nobody is going to laugh when they show up for the first day of school.

Then, we have to provide the school.

Beginners find the spark easier if they meet success soon after dipping their toes in the water. In this case, success is defined by getting bites or catching something when they go fishing, and at least having close encounters with animals when they go hunting. In target shooting, success is defined as regularly hitting what they're aiming at.

Fishing and hunting are about pursuit and capture. Secondary, and not unimportant, are fresh air and shared experiences. The secondary attractions of hunting and fishing keep you content down through the years, but only after you have experienced a measure of success. Too often, veteran hunters and anglers who take out newcomers bank on the power of fresh air and quality time for turning beginners into participants.

Reality: those secondary features are not enough by themselves. It will always be true that you have to go every time to get in on the good times. Most of us have heard the old sayings, about how it's called fishing and not catching, hunting and not harvesting. You cannot guarantee success. We all understand that. But let's face the truth about what it's like to be a beginner. Say all you want about quality time and beautiful sunrises in the duck marsh, but if a newcomer watches three straight sunrises without experiencing what it's like to hold still as ducks turn to the call, wings transform into perfect curves and orange feet stick out like landing gear, the newcomer can be excused for thinking that video games are more fun. (In the case of adult beginners, they will remember that there are 'more important' things they should be doing, or that one of their existing hobbies is more fun.)

When a seasoned hunter or angler thinks about what they love, freezing their butt off while nothing happens does not make the list. In order to help beginners find the flame, we should quickly teach them essential basics before they go, then build on them in the field. To further tip the odds for early success, all mentors should understand at least the basics of whatever specific type of fishing or hunting they are helping beginners try.

Even allowing for weather and the ability of anything with fins, fur, or feathers to make itself scarce, I believe that something good should happen by the end of a beginner's third outing.

Beginning hunters don't have to make the shot or even hold

still long enough to let a shooting situation fully develop, but they should have close encounters. Beginning anglers don't have to set the hook in time, and if the fish gets off it can actually make the story better. But hours on the water without a bite are easier to swallow after you've been bitten yourself. That's the first challenge: to inspire beginners, of all ages, to try hunting or fishing, and to help them experience success (as we are defining it here) quickly– before they decide it's boring, cold, wet, uncomfortable, or all of the above.

Then, if these first outings fan the flame (these sports are not for everybody), we have to continue creating chances for these beginners to find the aspects of fishing and/or hunting that they like best. (We also have to realize many people are going to like shooting as a sport unto itself, apart from hunting, and help them enjoy it as a hobby.)

Some people will discover that they love fly fishing for trout, or sunfish, or making a million casts in hopes of catching a big muskie. Maybe they will be drawn to the pursuit of big whitetail bucks, or the challenge of calling up a wild turkey. Maybe it's crappies. Who the heck knows ahead of time. People are individuals, and when it comes to their hobbies, they should do what they want to do.

Options will be dictated mainly by whatever is available locally, as the seasons change. Very few people have the time and money to zoom off to one dream destination after another. Let's say you are a prospective beginner. If you live in Texas, you might try fishing for bass or redfish, and you might try hunting for doves, deer, or turkeys. If you live in New York it could be salmon on the Great Lakes and deer hunting, or maybe it's public transportation to the seashore where you learn to cast for stripers.

Whatever each newcomer comes to, the only way to get there is by going on an ongoing basis. The only way to help newcomers find what they're drawn to is to help them try a variety of outdoor sports, then let them decide. The concept of gathering up inner city youths and letting them catch panfish for a couple hours, so that the makers of fishing tackle can kneel beside them and have their pictures taken with the kids, right before they are released back to their non-fishing lives, stands little chance of turning most inner city youths into anglers. The ongoing part is missing, and it's more important than going once.

There used to be a natural system for bringing the next generation along, which developed on its own back when fishing and hunting were skills counted on for survival. That train left the station long before the one we are clinging to now. For most modern people, hunting and fishing are sports, which they might choose to try, among a long list of other hobby choices. This is reality, just like the reality that, in today's world, many beginners will never be introduced properly to hunting or fishing unless someone unrelated by blood offers to do it, and then does it. Not once, or once a year, but on an ongoing basis.

Even in the old system, there were weaknesses that become harder to recall as the rose colored glasses get rosier with time. For one thing, there was a huge range of quality from instructor to instructor. You were handed one by fate. It wasn't all peaches and cream. Some 'instructors' did nothing more helpful than going fishing and hunting like they always had, and if the youngens could keep up without scaring anything away, they were allowed to remain with the group. If one of the youngens decided to quit, nobody sent out a press release or even helped them untie their boots. In those days, internal motivation among beginners was more necessary than it should have to be now, because today's mentors should be loaded up with whatever skills and knowledge they need to do the job well.

As long as we're dealing in reality, let's toss in the understanding that not every current sportsman is going to want to see this happen. For some members of the club it's all about secrecy; it's more important for some people to take their hard-won knowledge to the grave than offer it to somebody they don't know–especially if training newcomers means more competition for good spots. Plenty of people talk a good game about how we need more hunters and anglers, then turn into the biggest whiners when they pull up to the boat ramp and it's already full.

The modern landscape has changed in more ways than one. Another very real concern is that adults unrelated by blood taking kids into the field are susceptible to claims (by either the kids or their guardians) that something unbecoming happened out there when nobody was watching. Good people can be dragged through the mud in exchange for offering to help. Bad people can also pretend to be good people, slip skillfully through the background check, and use the new system for their own devices until, or unless, they get caught.

So this proposed new system won't be all peaches and cream, either. But none of this is grounds to give up. Today's beginners can actually stand a better chance of getting a good teacher, because it's easier to match up people willing to teach with those who want to try. Think eHarmony for fishing and hunting. Rather than playing violins and singing a sad song about the aging population of hunters, we should celebrate and recruit the bumper crop of experienced hunters who have lost the twinkle in their eye. Those old guys who don't go hunting as often as they used to, because they have conquered the challenges of their own youth, can be lured back. Their knees hurt early in the morning, they don't "hate the deer as bad as they used to," but I believe in my heart that they can rediscover hunting (or fishing) through the eyes of beginners–even beginners who are not their own grandchildren. Let's offer these veterans an important position in the new system, and help them transfer the fading twinkle in their own eyes to new members of the club.

Among willing adults who could use a little more knowledge and skill before assuming the role of instructor, let's embrace optimism and realize we can teach the teachers better than we used to. For one thing, both teacher and beginner have better equipment available to them than any generation ever. For another thing, it's easier to provide written, spoken and video lessons that the teacher can absorb before passing them on. For building the next generation of hunters and anglers, video games and the Internet (often thought of as chief enemy) can be harnessed as a huge asset.

All of this can be used to improve the quality of training offered by mentors who still fit the definition of the old system, too. If you are part of this 'old guard' and part of a classic family with kids and grandkids, you could probably use some assistance getting the youngsters to want to try fishing or hunting. And, despite all your years in the field, it would be nice to brush up on the details. Or get insights into an aspect of fishing or hunting you haven't tried, when your charges ask to try it.

Bits and pieces of this have been described, but as we sit here right now, we remain tangled in rhetorical questions about how to increase participation in traditional outdoor sports. If you already love to fish, hunt, or shoot targets, you know that a lot of other people are missing the boat. If you manufacture and sell equipment to anglers, hunters, and/or shooters, at least slowing the rate of decline in participation is the defining challenge of the times.

Here is the vision for a practical plan that will make a real difference:

- We inspire within beginners (of all ages) the desire to try these sports.

- We inspire within experienced hunters and anglers the desire to help beginners, and give them a way to do it.

- We train willing mentors who need lessons themselves, so they can lead beginners to success.

- We work within today's constraints, which are very real, when mentors unrelated by blood take kids into the field. Despite all obstacles, we match up beginners with mentors.

- We support ongoing outings for these beginners and mentors, so beginners can discover what aspects of these sports they like best.

Each outing does not have to be a grandiose event. It's better, in fact, if it's not. Our sports are best practiced by a quiet and loosely affiliated army. Beginners should be encouraged to find what they like, by trying everything that sounds fun. Through this process, beginners will become actual, active hunters, anglers, and shooters. This formula can create a steady stream of new participants.

All is far from lost, if we can pull ourselves away from old photo albums long enough to take part in the next sunrise. I like old stories as much as anybody does, and I believe history teaches us how to avoid making the same mistakes, when the current situation is fundamentally similar to the past. But in the case of fishing and hunting's future, we're on a new lake and there's no map of it.

To take a picture, you must deal with documenting reality as it exists.

To paint a picture, you can imagine what might be and create it.

I am the classic case of somebody who came to these sports through the old system, but I think we need to set up and run a new system. No more sitting around the station talking about how great it used to be, or only discussing the future in the context of wondering what can be done.

Let's turn and face the next sunrise.

Better yet: let's paint the next sunrise.

18

Chapter 3:
Outdoor Skills

In order to catch something when you go fishing, to have a close encounter with game when you go hunting, to hit what you aim at, there are things you need to know and things you need to do, often just at the right time.

Outdoor skills are the secrets to success. We must teach them to beginners, so these sports are given a sporting chance to fascinate them.

There's an old joke that's been tossed around by guides and outfitters about guaranteed hunts and guaranteed fishing trips. Before people pay to play, they sometimes ask, for example, whether a hunt is guaranteed. What the customer is asking: if *I pay you x amount of money, will you guarantee me a big deer?*

"Absolutely, it's a guaranteed hunt," is the standard response. "You're guaranteed to go hunting." Everybody gets a good laugh, especially any other guides or outfitters who happen to be within earshot.

If you've ever watched what good guides and outfitters go through while trying to create quality hunts for their customers, it's easy to get the joke. Many average hunters cannot sit still at crucial times, don't shoot accurately, are not experienced at seeing the game in order to set up for the shot, and don't have the same degree of stamina as the guide. In a lot of cases, a guide has to create three or four chances before the customer even gets the shot off. If the customer manages to get the shot off, accuracy of said shot is often marginal.

So how can we blame guides and outfitters for letting off a little steam when somebody asks whether a hunt is guaranteed? What hunt is ever guaranteed? What fishing day is ever guaranteed? Experienced hunters and anglers know that anything with fins, fur, or feathers has final control. Just about the time you think you understand even one of these creatures you are reminded that you don't know much of anything, because they do something you're positive they would never do.

Despite all this, it's my belief that beginners need to experience success early on, so they can decide whether hunting, fishing or target shooting is something they'd like to stick with. I'd like to see us guarantee something to everybody who decides to give our sports a try: that they will be given free access to easily-understood lessons, which will give them a sporting chance of success (as defined in Chapter 2) by the end of their third outing.

Those beginners who are paired, by chance, with a skilled and good teacher, stand an excellent chance of success. But even those beginners are subject to the whims of weather and everything else that can go wrong during pursuit of wild animals. That deer knows every sight, sound, and smell that it encounters on an everyday basis, so it's not exactly a secret when we show up, unless we're good at sneaking into position and remaining undetected. That deer does not need permission to run over to the neighbor's property, where we do not have permission to hunt. If the deer notices something is different, it doesn't have to know what it is. The deer can choose to lay there all day, moving around only at night.

There will always be plenty of challenges, even when a beginner is just trying to knock over a can with a .22 caliber rifle. Anybody who becomes a real hunter, shooter or angler needs to come to terms with the challenges, learn to at least put up with them, and hopefully learn to enjoy them along with all the benefits, including fresh air and sunrises. Eventually, real anglers come to understand that there is no such thing as a guarantee, helping them appreciate how sweet it is when they hook a big fish and, somehow, nothing goes wrong. The line does not break, the knot stays tied, the hook stays hooked, the line comes unwrapped from the log all by itself, and that big fish is at the boatside where it can be touched. (Hardcore anglers talk about getting to "touch the fish," which is code for, "I caught it, but didn't keep it.") Eventually, real hunters understand the same things, including how unbelievable it is when the deer turns and offers a perfect shot after getting away twenty-nine times in a row.

Seeing the fish for the first time, having it boil the water around your lure, fooling it enough to take a swipe, is what you should hope for as a beginner. Seeing the deer, even at a distance, is what you should hope for as a beginner.

As for the rest of it, see 'guarantee' above and try to laugh along with the rest of us, when things go as they often do, when you visit the places where animals live and try to pull the wool over their eyes.

Tipping the odds toward success is what we should strive for. Helping beginners feel what we feel is the only chance we have of creating a transfer of passion. The truth is, there are secrets to success. There are skills that can be called upon when knees are shaking and the excitement level goes through the roof. It's time to set up a system that teaches these skills, in language that's easy to understand, even if you've never done any of it before.

There is something missing, as big as a Montana sky, when we allow beginners to go into the field without enough advance knowledge, then rationalize their lack of success by talking about fresh air and quality time.

There have been actual revolutions in both hunting and fishing techniques in the past fifty years, and the equipment is better than ever. There is no shortage of how-to information if you seek the latest wrinkle, if you know where to look and have the knowledge to grasp it.

That last sentence reveals what is missing, when it comes to bringing newcomers along. There is no easily accessible, easily understood elementary school that holds hands and walks beginners from zero knowledge to a grasp of the basics. It takes time to know a good gap in the weeds when you see one, and a degree of skill to fire a cast just beyond the right place, then pause and twitch a bait through the sweet spot. It takes knowledge (experience helps also) to know when it might be a good time of day, or time of year, to quickly run a lipless crankbait across vast mid-depth flats, knowing that fish should be up there and ready to eat. It takes a degree of knowledge to make a good guess as to whether you should troll, cast, drift, anchor up, or dead-stick.

It takes knowledge to read that last sentence and even know what it means.

It takes experience to know when you should try to move up on a gobbling turkey and when you should hang back and let him come to you. It takes experience to know when (and where) to move the goose decoys because the wind shifted. Ditto for whether you should hang in there or move the stand, if you're not seeing any deer.

Before you can attempt an accurate cast into a gap in the weeds, it helps to understand what a fishing rod is, how it should be balanced with the reel, what role the line plays, how much line to leave hanging off the tip as you begin the casting motion, when to let your thumb off the spool, and more. Before you can hope to get close enough to bugle in an elk, you have to learn how to walk quietly in the woods, what movement you can and can't get away with, when you have to hold absolutely still, and more.

And lest we give off the impression that there is always a 'correct' move or decision to make, beginners need to know that most hunting and fishing situations put you in the position of having to make decisions (move or stay put, call or don't, etc.), and there are usually multiple decisions that could lead to success. The wisest hunters and anglers make decisions, try something that makes sense, then accept what happens. If the game gets away–actually, when the game gets away, because it happens constantly–they live with it. They laugh about it. They tip their hat to the wild animal that got away again.

Beyond the basics, the list of things beginners need to know, and need to know how to do, is endless. But if we do a good job of teaching the core basics to all beginners, if we help them feel the excitement of hunting and fishing, they will stick around long enough to figure out whether they like to fish bass or trout, and whether they would choose deer hunting over duck hunting, or like all of it, changing what they do as the seasons come and go.

If we teach the basics well, we will have succeeded, and each beginner will choose what endless pile of details to dig into.

Getting people to that point is where we are failing.

Chapter 4:
A Good Place to Go

**To get anywhere in hunting, fishing, or target
shooting, you have to find a good place to go.**

Here, in the issue of access, we uncover a natural conflict among
fellow hunters and anglers. Those of us who already hunt and fish
are veterans in the competition for good spots, and it's intense if
you don't have money to trade for a honey hole. Even if we don't
bring any new people into these sports, it feels like there aren't
enough good spots to go around.

So whose great idea is it, to add more hunters and anglers, all of
whom are hoping to find a good place to go? It can be a bit of a
double-edged sword, but the survival of our sports depends upon a
steady flow of newcomers, who eventually replace current players.

Creatures at the top of the food chain need a lot of room to operate, which can imperil their very survival. If you're a grizzly bear or timber wolf, you want, and are willing to fight for, a large territory over which to roam and hunt. It isn't the same thing, but hunters and anglers also need room to operate, multiple places to search for what they are trying to catch or kill.

If you're a deer hunter, in your perfect world you're the only one allowed to hunt on a huge tract of prime land. In the real world, most hunters rarely secure exclusive permission to hunt big blocks of ground. In the real world, plenty of hunters exclusively hunt public land, where there is never-ending and unpredictable competition for the best areas. On private or public places, many hunters spend considerable time scouting deer movements and set up numerous stands to choose from, depending on which way the wind is blowing. Nothing ticks them off more than sneaking into one of those stands and finding another hunter already sitting in it.

The borders of private property often feature deer stands that face meadows on the neighbor's place, and there isn't even the pretense that whoever is sitting in those stands will be watching their own land while scanning for an animal to shoot at. Substitute an image of duck or pheasant hunters who covet undisturbed wild spaces, where they can play their favorite sport. Substitute two trout fishermen who bump into each other while eyeing up a good-looking stretch, or two boats that slide onto the same redfish flat looking for the same thing.

Even on public property, including public waters, feelings of possessiveness are common.

The hope that other people will never find your 'secret' spot will never go away, but we should try to share. We should try to want to share. It typically takes a hunter or angler many years to arrive at this sense of peace and willingness to share spots, but access equals opportunity, and access is necessary for beginners to feel the magic. When most people talk about the modern issue of access, they are speaking of No Trespassing signs. To me, there is great potential to ease the access dilemma by inviting beginners to come with you to land you have permission to hunt, and to waters you know hold decent fish. It is proper etiquette for those beginners to then look for their own spots, in order to avoid competing with you in the future. But taking them to good spots helps them get off to a good start.

Let's come right out and say it: even hunters and anglers who swear they are all for getting more people involved in hunting and fishing are protective of their favorite spots. Getting newcomers started is a pet project for me, yet this conflict resides within me, too; I'm guilty of feeling competitive when there's a gobbling turkey and along comes some other camo-clad guy I don't know who wants to set up on that same bird.

Increasingly, on our finite landscape, there is competition for prime places to pursue fish and game. The issue of access is a huge obstacle as we attempt to create a bright future for hunting and shooting (and, to a lesser degree, fishing).

Jerry McGinnis, longtime TV show host, told me one time at a sports show that he did not like to film fishing shows on exclusive waters. Because he was on the inside and had his own show, he would receive invitations to bring the cameras and enjoy the bounty of private ponds and other waters off limits to the average Joe. He talked about politely declining such invitations. "I don't want to do a show," he said, "on a place where you can't go, next weekend."

Amen.

The issue of access is going to get nothing but harder to resolve. But I would argue that, even if it means further increasing the difficulty, more hunters and anglers are the best friends that wild animal populations, and the planet, can hope for. We've all heard this, but it's absolutely true that hunters and anglers have historically paid the lion's share for habitat and game management, and have often led the charge for legislation aiming to preserve or improve water and air quality. Because our sports are played in wild places, we have a vested interest in maintaining the playgrounds.

There won't be a perfect answer to the issue of access, but we're better off if more of us love to fish, hunt, and shoot. We briefly mentioned this, but it's probably going to be necessary to redefine the experience, especially in the case of hunting. Most outings for most hunters, in the modern world, are going to take place on 'semi-wild' land close to houses and other development. Clinging to the desire for large, exclusive, wild playgrounds will, indeed, further imperil the survival of our sports. Most modern hunters will have to settle for occasional trips into spots remote and vast, finding satisfaction in regular outings of a more humble nature.

Even in a smaller garden, we can still find, and learn to share, the fun.

Chapter 5:
See Everything

One of the great joys of being a hunter or an angler is that you get to spend time in wild places. Some of them, you see only once. Others are close to home, and they become special because you go there often and know their secrets.

Hunting and fishing, like a good story, can be experienced and enjoyed on many levels.

When you go on your own adventures, take time to see everything.

Silence of the Windy Wheat

When the wind blows on the prairie, the clatter drowns all other sounds, until you don't hear much of anything. But there's plenty to see, out to the curvature of the earth. It can be hard to tell what's bigger, the sky or the endless waving grass.

The colors are worth noticing, even if it all looks brown at first glance. It isn't. There's white, rust, copper, and the toughest shades of silver and black you'll ever come across. The wild prairie is merciless at times, and that's probably why more people don't live out here. Peaceful, even when it's forceful, and one of the greatest places to hunt birds if you love to unleash a good dog and let the dog take you hunting.

If you read magazine articles about how to successfully hunt upland game, tackling enormous tracts of prairie grass, one hunter, one dog, is exactly what they tell you not to attempt. Too much real estate, way too many escape options. Get on a bird, and you will probably cross from one habitat type to another before you either get a shot, watch it flush wild, or the bird gives you the slip. But in this type of pure pursuit, talented dogs learn their craft. In this ocean of possible hiding places you get to see the real game of cat and mouse, if you can control yourself, let the dog hunt, and do nothing more than stay in position and shoot when the time comes.

The chase, in this case, is more than fair.

One actual spot that defines this scenario, probably my favorite ever, is on the border between North Dakota and Saskatchewan. A good friend, Harold Reistad, drove me out there one afternoon many years ago, when I could walk farther and faster than I can now. We went separate directions and, dog whistle in his gnashing teeth, Harold said to meet at the truck when it was getting dark.

No matter how featureless you might consider the prairie to be, there are always distinctive landmarks. I remember making a mental note about an odd-shaped mound and small sodium lake that would help keep things straight. While I was still gathering up our bearings, my black lab Buddy led me up the first grassy hillside, we topped it, and that's when I saw all the way to Canada.

Along the crest of the next ridge he hit a bird, snapping me back into the hunt. Tight muscles, black shiny fur, then only glimpses of orange collar when the chase moved into waist-high cover.

A certain angle of his neck and head told me that we were closing. A few final, frantic changes of direction and Buddy stopped dead and stared into the grass. His tail twitched, but nothing else moved. The bird was right there and I could see him already, in my mind, because I knew what he was going to look like. The dog held long enough for me to walk in tight, and I released Buddy by saying, "Git 'im!" and the dog plunged forward and the bird's wings fought the cover, but fear of the canine teeth pushed it free, a beautiful rooster that flared its tail and swung up and to the right. The shot shattered the silence of the windy wheat, and the bird's momentum carried it, in a heap, to Buddy, who was running along underneath its flight.

I know that good trainers say your dog is supposed to sit at the flush and mark the bird down before being sent for the retrieve, but I've always had this thing about that. I want my dog to chase the bird I'm going to shoot at, like Willie Mays running and looking over his shoulder to track that long fly ball in the World Series, the famous basket catch. I want my dog to be on that bird when it goes down. If my dogs chase a hen, so be it, because by the time they do that a few times, it's easy to holler, "no bird" and call them off.

Do this over and over, together, and you become a team.

On this day, that first winding chase played out a dozen more times in the next couple hours. I shot one more rooster and went along for the ride on the others. Buddy kept jumping up out of his stance to watch long-tailed birds ride their wings until they blended with the background, and he kept looking back at me to see if I was still on the team.

At one point, Buddy was hot on a bird at the same time a flock of sandhill cranes was wheeling overhead. Even though I couldn't hear what they were singing, for the windy wheat, it was spectacular. At another point, a small flock of sharptails came flying directly at us, for whatever reason. Maybe they were moving from food to roost? Maybe they were chased into the air by a coyote? I hunkered down in the grass like I was hiding from approaching mallards. When the grouse got close enough I stood up and fired, but it was only a wave goodbye.

At 6 o'clock, we filled the air with more sharptails, from a place where the wheat met the grass. They got up just a little too far away and effortlessly rode those wings, washing with the wind until we couldn't see them anymore.

I've seen sharptails up close, and heard their clucking at the flush. This was better than that, and it was time to go find the truck.

Getting Hooked

Sometimes the water is so clear that it looks like you and the fish are part of the same world, which you are. Fishing can become a stabilizing force through all the changes in your life. No matter what, if you like to fish, there's always something to look forward to.

When I was a kid, I liked to sleep on a cot set out on the floating portion of the dock at our cabin on Lake of the Woods, rocking with the water and listening to loons and glimpsing falling stars that left vapor trails. I'd often wake up in the soft light before sunrise, stand on the edge of the dock and look for fish in the clear water.

Perch and rock bass would poke their dark heads out from between the cribs that supported the permanent dock. You could catch them on a tiny jig if you felt like it, like ice fishing in the summer. My brothers, sisters, and I used to do it for hours. My kids do it for hours now.

But there was also a huge fallen tree, now mostly gone, with a tangle of branches, a cast away from the side of the floating dock. It held bigger fish.

I remember well, one morning, picking up a rod rigged with a yellow spinnerbait (about the time spinnerbaits were invented, so they were the hot new thing). Even though I wasn't authorized to use that rod, I walked over and held it while studying the water around that sunken tree. I took the rod back and arced a cast beyond the tree that landed with a plunk, the first real sound of the day. I reeled the spinner just under the surface until it got over a crevice between two branches and let it flutter gently, dangerously, down.

The bait disappeared from view and, for the first time ever, I set the hook like I meant business, like I knew what I was doing. A firm, stubborn resistance came back, sort of the same feeling as being hung up, but I knew better, and the telltale shine of a fighting bass lit up the water around that tree. The battle moved out into open water, featured one good jump, but soon I clamped my thumb on the fish's lower jaw, unhooked it, and sent it back to the tree.

A little lightbulb went off in my head. I took the 14-foot boat around the corner to a bay guarded by a white whale rock entrance and pulled the boat up on shore. I walked around the edge of another island with my own rod, and used a CountDown Rapala (another hot, new bait at that time) to probe other sunken trees that I knew about. In my mind, I can still see the bait rocking left and right, as it dropped on a slack line between perilous underwater tree branches, and big smallmouths rising out of the darkness to take me for a ride.

Chapter 6:
What it Means to be a Hunter or Angler

Can you both value life and take it?

You can if you are a hunter.

Being a hunter, or angler, comes down to the essential difference between concern over animal populations and concern over one animal.

It must have torn my dad's insides out to watch me sitting there in the duck boat with a wounded mallard in my lap, holding it and thinking of it as a pet, asking if we could take it home and see if it would live.

The dog had brought it back alive and now the duck and I were sitting together on a seat cushion. My dad was splitting time between watching the sky for more ducks and looking down at me, while trying to come up with a strategy for handling the situation. He handled it like he handled most situations, by first letting it develop to see if I would change my mind; then, after about a half-hour, by sitting next to me and appealing to common sense about how the duck was not going to live for long and it wasn't practical to keep a duck in a cardboard box in the garage.

In the end, I let him finish it off, and watched to see how it was done.

I suppose I was about eight years old on that day, and it was a natural set of feelings, some of which have never left me. The final dispatch has never been something to celebrate in my mind, whether it's a pheasant in the field or a walleye at the fillet table.

No speech from me about how death is part of life, or how humans are innate hunters now repressed by modern society and the shrinking hunting grounds. When the subject of why we hunt comes up, lots of reasons are offered. At the core, hunting is innate, not just for humans but for all, because the search for something to eat and the quest to remain uneaten is never at rest.

The wilderness has been tamed, but it still tugs at a lot of us, and we try to justify wanting to leave our modern caves to go out hunting when we really wouldn't have to. You don't have to justify it to me, because I feel it too. Ted Nugent has said that we don't have to defend hunting, because there is nothing to defend, and he is right. Being a hunter feels right to those of us who feel this way, but possessing the power of taking has always come with responsibility. I worry about people who enjoy it too much or begin to itch in the trigger finger, who talk about needing to draw blood. Perhaps there is that, for some hunters or anglers, but we should all search the unwritten code to see that respect for any powers will always be the most important part of having them.

Let's talk about the differences between hunters and anti-hunters, anglers and anti-anglers.

Also, hunters and non-hunters, anglers and non-anglers.

Years ago, at an Outdoor Writers Association of America conference, Wayne Pacelle, a well-known spokesman for the anti-hunting movement, was in attendance. This caused controversy between people who believe in exploring differences and those who believe in keeping outsiders away from the clubhouse. At the time, I was writing and hosting a syndicated radio show, National Outdoors, so it was a multi-part series begging to be produced. I introduced myself to Mr. Pacelle and asked if he could make time for an interview.

That's what he was there for, so he agreed and we sat for more than an hour. I chose to lead the conversation along the search for common ground between hunters and anti-hunters. Mr. Pacelle was polite, extremely articulate, and made some concessions that there could be a bit of common ground, as long as hunters would be willing to abolish what he defined as particularly objectionable forms of hunting, such as baiting of bears.

After the interview, several outdoor writers came up to me with a mixture of messages, ranging from *how could you?* to *what did he have to say?* For that afternoon, I was stuck in the middle between the anti-hunting movement and members of my own team, simply for deciding to talk things over. The truth is that I don't personally believe Wayne Pacelle, or his fellow anti-hunters, would be content with small victories such as banning bear baiting, but would treat them as a foot in the door that, once cracked, could be used as leverage to try to end all forms of hunting. Still, having the discussion felt worthwhile. It was a respectful exchange between two people who could not be any further apart philosophically.

We aired a long series that year on the search for common ground.

Whether any other hunters have the stomach to sit down and talk with members of the anti-hunting movement is not the bigger point. At the very least, it's worth talking, in the interest of more clearly defining differences. Hunters and anti-hunters are not likely to ever find common ground, but the questions you have to ask yourself, if you struggle at all on this fence, will help you decide which side of the fence you're on. Or, whether you are content to straddle it.

To me, the difference between being a hunter or an anti-hunter comes down to an important distinction: the difference between being mainly concerned about individual animals or populations of animals. As with all issues that include an emotional component, there are plenty of details to ponder, including wondering how much real caring there is on either side if you disagree with it. (There is plenty of evidence that suggests the animal rights movement places more emphasis on raising money than actually protecting stray cats or worrying about the fate of timber wolves.) At the core, a hunter can live with killing individual animals, but works hard to protect the habitat in which animals live, and genuinely cares about the health of animal populations. This gets twisted and represented as hypocritical by those opposed to hunting. Modern hunters—who could easily have other people gather up food for them—get accused of supporting habitat protection and game management in the name of raising more targets solely so they can go out and kill the targets.

True hunters would not, should not, view game populations as triumph on the hoof, but should feel excited about the prospects of a successful hunt when there is a harvestable surplus of game around. The taking of game or fish can (commonly does) make the hunter or angler feel satisfaction and pride. But when the emotions spill over into feelings of superiority over taken animals, or superiority over fellow humans who are not as skilled at taking animals, selfishness has crept in where it doesn't belong.

Among a few people masquerading as hunters, there are motivations not at all in keeping with the sport. Heartless killers and poachers will always be a part of the human race, but they should not be called, or thought of as, hunters. They should be called what they are, a separate category, even when they have purchased a hunting license before going on a spree.

There is no contradiction in feeling privileged to be alive and be in a wild place in pursuit of wild game, then feel remorse and respect at the kill, all while feeling proud to be a hunter. Just as there is no contradiction in eating the meat from the kill and showing your friends pictures of the dead animal at the site of the kill, and caring about what happens to the land upon which this wild creature lived and working toward perpetuating the cycle of life and death, all while smack in the middle of it, washing blood off your own hands from time to time.

There is a huge difference between being opposed to hunting and making a decision that it's just not for you. If you believe the pollsters (which I do), a small percentage of Americans are anti-hunters, a slightly larger percentage are hunters, and a majority are non-hunters who remain comfortable with the notion that some of us still go out hunting.

So that's where we are right now, a growing human population living on a planet that cannot be expanded. Some of us want to keep hunting and fishing, some of them try to get us to stop, and still others are deciding whether hunting or fishing might be fun to try. People have always had to share space with others who disagree with them on important issues, but as our population grows, it becomes harder to find a neutral corner.

How each of us feels about taking animal life is not a simple question, but for most people it is an understandable one that they can form an opinion on fairly quickly. For those of us who are hunters or anglers, or who might be interested, it is a doorway we must pass through in order to arrive at one side or the other. Can we both value life and take it? Regardless of whether we feel remorse at the moment of kill or most alive in that moment, true hunters and anglers feel respect hand in hand with excitement and pride. True hunters and anglers become interested in working for the good of animal populations and the health of the planet all life depends on.

Pretty simple. And extremely complex. No room for selfishness, no matter what side of the fence we're on. And we could use more respect for each other, as we all make personal choices.

Chapter 7:
How Good Does it Have to Be?

How good does the fishing or hunting have to be, in order for us to find excitement and satisfaction in it?

This is an important question every hunter and angler should ask.

Success, and accompanying satisfaction, can be found in the definition of both.

Do you have to catch big ones every time out? Do you have to 'maximize' your potential as an angler, in order to find the fun in fishing? Do you have to shoot a big buck every fall, or a mature gobbler with long spurs every spring, or risk losing what you seek from the hunt?

This is the tangled mess many anglers and hunters allow themselves to become ruled by. Success, as defined by catching the most and the biggest fish or shooting the buck with the grandest antlers, becomes the primary ruler of too many minds. Reputations, ego, and pride become tied to consistently pursuing and capturing bragging-board animals.

In too many cases, that's how human nature works.

It's good to be competitive, as long as that drive does not consume the part of your brain able to appreciate hunting and fishing as pursuits not always ending in capture. You have probably heard the old saying about how the sun doesn't shine on the same dog's rear end every day. For our purposes here, it means that the same angler is not going to catch a big fish every day, and the same hunter is not going to bag a big buck every season.

As is often the case, communications tied to selling fishing and hunting equipment are partly to blame. Advertising professionals keep lists of all the emotions they might appeal to, in order to get you to want a new gun even though your old one still works. They know your weaknesses. Professional anglers and hunters, paid to promote the latest lures or guns, are presented in marketing messages as gods among men, who can go forth under any conditions and return with the most difficult game in hand. Outdoor television shows are edited in order to make it appear that the host catches big fish way more often than anybody you know. Human nature being what it is, you buy the stuff those guys endorse, and push yourself harder in an effort to measure up.

There are good and bad aspects of human nature, and the selfish desire to be admired for consistently catching big fish or bagging big deer is one of the bad ones. We have to look selfish desires straight in the eyeballs, recognize them, and keep them at bay. There is a huge difference between feeling overjoyed when a big buck steps out and you make the shot, and deciding that it should happen all the time from now on–that shooting this year's big buck is necessary for perpetuating your status in the hunting hierarchy.

Putting pressure on yourself to bag a bird or 'nail' a big fish can easily become all-consuming. Even if you do consistently bag fish and game, don't kid yourself: there are plenty of other people who also do it, many of whom do not take pictures of every triumph. The catch or kill should not be used as padding for human egos and reputations–or become the driving force behind continued participation.

Wishing too much for yourself also endangers the ability to celebrate honestly for other people when they catch a big fish or the big buck steps out in front of them. Being able to feel just as excited for somebody else, if it doesn't come naturally, is worth working on.

Being able to truly enjoy each outing for what it brings is also worth working on. Yes, we can probably all agree that it's more fun when we get something, but if we are to chart a bright future for hunting and fishing–as the human population grows and wilderness areas become less common–we have to redefine, in fundamental ways, what it means to be successful out there.

Average hunters and anglers, as we have already said, are not going to spend most of their days in dream destinations. Most outings are going to take place on the fringes of modern life, where finite numbers of average size animals make up the complete list of what we can hope to capture, no matter how good our skills or how lucky we are.

If we are to chart a bright future for hunting and fishing, more of us have to find satisfaction in helping beginners develop skills and find their first successes. It begins with accepting the truth: catching fish and killing game animals should not be something we do in order to make ourselves feel better or more important. Consider the possibility that it might feel even better to watch somebody else land their first five-pound bass, than for you to 'nail' your three hundredth five-pound bass.

We should want to cheer for each other! My dad taught me that, and it's one of his finest legacies. When one person in your camp shoots a nice deer, or somebody in the next boat catches a nice fish, check with yourself. Are you mainly wishing that was you? Or are you genuinely happy for the person upon whose rear end the sun is shining today? Unless you have your own television show and can control the filming and editing of it, it's difficult to make it appear as if you catch a big one on every cast. The reality is that luck plays a fairly large part, if we all learn the same skills and all have access to pretty much the same grounds on which to hunt and fish.

So how good does it have to be?

The extent to which you take your personal skills, and personal quest, is up to you. There is nothing wrong with being obsessed with hunting and fishing to the point that they become your main hobbies, or even the source of your livelihood. Go for it, especially if you feel pulled by it. Hone your skills to pattern and harvest big whitetail bucks, or tempt and land big bass.

But selfishness is in control if you hope your prowess will lead to other people worshipping the ground you walk on. There are professional hunters and anglers, people who give seminars and appear on television shows, and sign autographs at sports shows. All of that is good, as long as it remains in perspective.

How good does the fishing have to be, in order for most of us to find the fun and want to keep doing it? Not that good, really. Just good enough that we can catch some fish on purpose most of the time and, occasionally, have a crack at a big one.

Accept the big ones, when they come, for the great gift they are. Treat them with respect, and feel humbled for having caught them–not triumphant or more important.

How good does the hunting have to be, really?

If we look honestly in the mirror, we all know the answer.

Chapter 8:
Keepers of Every Flame

It's not enough to say that, some day, you plan on bringing a beginner fishing, hunting, or shooting. If you have at least the basic qualifications necessary to be a mentor, you should honor the tradition and fan the flame, on an ongoing basis.

The old guard–current anglers and hunters–has a particularly urgent responsibility at this crucial moment in hunting and fishing history.

Some of us can feel it at the beginning of the day, boots and brush pants pressing through the edges as we close the gun and talk the dog in tighter because all that energy is unleashed to chase birds that don't want to be caught. We can feel it because we've been there before and know what's coming next.

Some of us can feel it as the sun rises red over the trees, the lake in front of us, and we can see, in our minds, below the reflective surface as the shoreline drops away into twenty feet on the depthfinder. We drive across the basin toward the edges of a hump that might be holding fish right now. Waves crashing against the side of the boat find their way, in a spray, to the side of our face, and the taste reminds us of what it will feel like to have a fish on.

This is how it is for people who should be keepers of the flame.

Newcomers tagging along on the hunt, or riding beside us in the boat, feel something very different. The grass makes their pants wet, and the water off the side of the boat simply splashes them in the face, and they turn away. But if we take them along more than once, and help them experience success, many beginners will make their own connections with wild places and sports of pursuit.

Connections are waiting to be made. Yes, there are obstacles, but there always are. A big one is the tendency to insulate ourselves from ever getting too cold, too hot, or splashed in the face on purpose.

Many of us, even lifelong participants, are losing connection with the earth and our sports. Fewer newcomers are joining our ranks. The traditional outdoor sports are in great danger of shriveling, perhaps even dying. The time has come for more of us, no matter how private we are about our outings, to share them with others so that the flame gets passed before it goes out.

Again, we're not talking about once-a-year, highly promoted events. This is all about creating chances for beginners, of all ages, to go fishing, hunting, or shooting, away from the crowds, on a regular basis.

A quiet army is needed to be keepers of the flame. First, we need a way to awaken, within potential beginners, a latent desire to try fishing and hunting–and to fulfill strong desires that already exist. At the same time, we must inspire, among accomplished hunters and anglers, a lasting commitment to share what are often quiet and personal outings.

Then, finally, we must find a way to match up prospective beginners with willing teachers. To help them all grow in skills, which leads to regular success. To help them understand that mastery over these sports, as defined by the harvesting of fish and game, is not the ultimate triumph. Through the process, they will be nudged toward realization that we, the people, are supposed to be the keepers of every flame.

During the course of modern hunting and fishing history, wildlife managers have taken rough measurements of hunter and angler proficiency. Those measurements have been used to estimate how much pressure 'the resource' can handle. It's not difficult to find wildlife managers who think hunters and anglers are already too effective, and it's not uncommon to hear inferences that the last thing we need are more, and more widespread, improvements in skill level. If we subscribe to the notion that humans are essentially selfish, it's easy to imagine that arming more people with lethal levels of technique will bring wildlife populations to a methodical demise. The notion is that, if everybody knows how to catch fish and shoot game on a consistent basis, we won't be able to help ourselves. We'll kill everything until there's nothing left.

That's one way to think about it, but I say hogwash. I say there's no pretend victory in trying to poke the how-to genie back into the bottle. I say we teach everybody the same things, the best methods ever developed for hunting and fishing success. I say that with consistent success will come less fervor to kill, not more. Yes, there will be exceptions, but I choose to believe humans are essentially good and that, on balance, successful hunters and anglers go afield more often and serve as front line stewards of natural resources.

To save our sports, we have to create the help beginners–and mentors–need, to fuel their ongoing adventures, by demystifying the secrets to being successful. Success can become the norm, for most participants. As keepers of the flame, we should also help newcomers progress quickly through the recognized phases hunters and anglers go through, so they feel confident success can be repeated regularly. That places responsible stewardship within emotional grasp of most people, so that iffy shots are passed on and plenty of nice fish are released alive.

This becomes possible when you believe you can repeat the success next time.

In the relationship between predator and prey, our human place can be centered in the crosshairs, elevating the ranks of hunters and anglers in the process. Only in recent times has it become common for hunters to be on camera at the moment of making a kill, and fishermen at the moment a catch comes over the bow. Too often, this face time has brought out conquering behavior not in keeping with the spirit our sports should stand for. Conquering heroes may have, in times long past, been part of hunting and fishing, when success meant something to eat. True keepers of the traditional flame in today's world are content to provide chances for someone new to pull the trigger or set the hook. Just as importantly, they serve as role models who demonstrate the right way to celebrate each capture.

In fact, a true keeper of the flame becomes motivated mainly by these desires.

Chapter 9:
A Bright Future for Outdoor Sports

It's always painful to break a comfortable old mold and make a new one, but that's what we have to do in order to intervene on behalf of fishing, hunting, and recreational shooting. This should be a natural path in this case, though, on the new social landscape with its changing family structures, and in the digital age, where video, audio, and text can be offered up, free of charge, for the common good.

A casual look over the bow at current participation in these sports, and current trends in participation, paints a disheartening picture. Fewer people are fishing, hunting, and shooting for fun. We have arrived at a point in time and combination of circumstances that conspire to chip away at the traditions and eventually relegate them to obscurity and insignificance. It would be easy to throw our hands up in resignation, to allow current forces to deposit the legacies of these sports wherever the winds of modern society blow them. Yet, for all the challenges, there is a simultaneous perfect storm that can be harnessed to breathe life into these activities.

These are traditions worthy of preserving, with a relevance, perhaps more now than ever, given the finite nature of Nature and the history of sportsmen and women volunteering to protect it. Going into wild places for recreation inevitably provides fabulous bonuses: perspective, reflection, a sense of purpose, a classic recharging of the human spirit.

The old paradigm was formed when things were different. Nowadays, someone interested in becoming a beginner is less likely to know someone who can (and will) show them the ropes. Absent a vibrant old system, we have to create a new one. Absent, in many people's lives, the classic related-by-blood, in-the-flesh mentor, we can build a virtual bridge between beginners and what they need to know. The solution, in fact, can prop up weaknesses in the old system. Nobody's uncle has ever been knowledgeable in everything the nephews and nieces wanted to try, so beginners wound up going perch fishing if that's what their uncle knew how to do.

Any sweat equity we pour into setting up a new system will also create long overdue equality of opportunity. The entrenched system has always resulted in more opportunity for boys than girls and has always favored youngsters over adult beginners. In our proposed new system, girls will be treated the same as boys. Adults and children will be treated equally.

There is hope where there is opportunity for all.

Computers and Internet as Solution

Because we can, and because it will work, we should use the same technology blamed for tearing us away from the outdoors to deliver basic lessons in anything and everything anybody might ever want to try. Then, helpful experts, versed in the basics, should be standing by, ready to use this same technology to answer follow-up questions.

Put this fundamental belief to the test: it's my contention that we can tell anybody 80 percent of what they need to know about any aspect of these sports in a couple hours, doing the explaining in simple words, illustrated with pictures. Further, it's my contention that we can build a school of outdoor sports and house it on the Internet, and reach out from there to people without Internet access.

It's time to create the elementary school where beginners, of all ages, are quickly taught essential basics, in the name of pouring more active participants onto the landscape. The world will be a better place when more people spend more time outdoors. This is worth doing even if it makes it more difficult to find a good place to hunt or fish; more outdoorsmen and women mean more advocates for wild places, healthy shooting sports, and a thriving customer base for products and services related to these pursuits.

Blame computers all you want for being chief enemy, or imagine them as primary weapon, powerful and effective as a scoped-and-sighted rifle, driving tacks that ignite sparks that get more people out there in the fields and on the water. In the new system, you won't need to know anybody ahead of time, in order to get off to the right start and keep going.

A Quiet Army

History has taught us that the ranks of anglers and hunters are dominated by people who prefer to take quiet outings away from fanfare. Success, in fact, is usually directly proportional to how much distance you put between yourself and the rest of the world.

It has always been difficult to rally groups of hunters and anglers to attend meetings or unify their voice on behalf of a cause. This is a natural dynamic we should cater to, rather than attempting to change it. The more 'official' anything related to the outdoors becomes, the more many anglers and hunters slip back into the shadows, where they feel most comfortable.

It appears to me that we have a perfect storm fully brewed, waiting for us to harness its powers. Again, because it's possible, we should use the Internet to assemble and assist a quiet army that takes quiet outings, breathing new life into these traditions. We should create a virtual lodge where members of this quiet army can sit in front of the virtual fireplace and share stories and pictures from time afield.

The atmosphere in this virtual lodge needs to be welcoming and inclusive, an ingredient often in short supply in many existing web-based forums where hunters and anglers gather. (Too often, a not-so-subtle hint that "we know something you don't and never will" permeates the gathering places of experienced anglers and hunters, and this is not confined to online gatherings.) In this new setting, where the ground rules establish that no question is too basic, frequently asked queries will be handled with patience and style, no matter how many times the same questions come up.

Beginner-mentor match-ups will flourish, whether they are naturally created by family ties or through more formal mechanisms.

This new school of outdoor sports will not function as a mentoring organization, but will work strategically with existing mentoring groups to help facilitate additional match-ups. A shining example is Pass It On Outdoor Mentors, begun in 1999 in Kansas and now serving a growing list of states. Led by energetic, optimistic, dedicated Mike Christensen, this group uses the model refined by Big Brothers Big Sisters to match up eager beginners with willing mentors, then supports ongoing activities centered around the outdoors.

(If you are ready to be a mentor, or know a youngster who wants to be matched up, check it out at www.outdoormentors.org.)

Partnerships will be important among this elementary school, mentoring groups, and other existing efforts to introduce newcomers. After a kid goes out on youth waterfowl day, somebody needs to keep that youngster going after youth waterfowl day is over.

In time, a stream of beginners will pass through the school and become a flow of new participants that chips away at the declining rate of participation. Each beginner starts with whatever strikes his or her fancy, but there are many possible roads to go down. These are lifetime sports, and a lifetime is a long time. Even active participants are likely to try a new road every now and then. The school will patiently dish out essential basics, on any subject, for anyone, at any time.

It's unrealistic to hope that every outing results in bounty, but if we break down every barrier to success and exploration, and all beginners are allowed to decide for themselves what they like best, a happy ending can be snatched from the jaws of demise.

Here's the vision: School of Outdoor Sports

Only recently has Internet technology progressed to the point that it became feasible and reasonable to put moving pictures and sound on web sites. Now, it's possible to create and post basic video lessons on fishing, hunting, and shooting. In conjunction with these lessons, online forums can allow beginners to ask follow-up questions and get helpful clarifications.

With this in mind, a nonprofit organization has been founded, dedicated to increasing participation in these outdoor sports.

Getting past the intimidation factor and learning curve have forever limited the exploration of beginners in these activities. There has never been one place where beginners are offered the keys to any door they feel like cracking, just to see if it might be their new favorite hobby.

Now, there will be.

In short order, a 'student' can learn most of what he or she needs to know, from an overall standpoint, in one of three broad categories: fishing, hunting, or shooting. For example, let's say you are interested in fishing. First, you watch a video that teaches you most of what you will ever need to know, regardless of what species of fish you're trying to catch.

That grounds you in overall basics. Then you choose a certain type of fishing–let's say bass fishing–and you watch another video that teaches you most of what you need to know about bass fishing. In a few hours, you are ready–truly ready–to try bass fishing. You still have to practice the skills, and if you are a youngster, you still need somebody to take you. But fear of the unknown is gone, replaced by excitement, confidence, expectations, possibilities.

You try bass fishing, and because you understand the basics, you catch a few without having to spend days catching nothing. Those initial experiences let you decide whether bass fishing is something you want to continue with. If bass fishing captures your imagination, a lifetime of details and wonder spread out in front of you. You now dream of buying a bass boat and you read fishing magazines and watch fishing shows. Suddenly, there are so many lures, so many lakes, and so little time.

But let's say, for whatever reason, bass fishing is not your cup of tea. You might want to try walleye fishing or crappie fishing instead. Back to the school you go, where you watch the basic lessons on walleye fishing or crappie fishing. The same potential lifelong attachment awaits, should one of those pursuits cling to you.

Let's say you want to try hunting. To the school you go, where you watch the video on the overall basics of hunting. Then you watch the one on deer hunting, and you are ready to give it a try. You still need state-mandated hunter safety training, but once you have certificate in hand, because you understand the basics you stand a decent chance of getting close enough to a deer to attempt a shot. You also stand a decent chance of making an accurate shot. That's how you discover whether deer hunting is for you.

Beyond deer hunting, you can choose to learn the basics of dove hunting, turkey hunting, pheasant hunting, duck hunting, goose hunting—whatever you want.

Let's say you are interested in target shooting. Spend time in the school, in the shooting area, and a lifetime of calibers, gauges, sighting systems and marksmanship games awaits.

This is all available to you, around the clock, any day of the year, free of charge.

Bowing to the reality that everyone cannot watch video on their computer—yet—discs can be sent through the mail. Also, these same lessons can be read, illustrated with still images, even on computers with turtle-slow, dial-up service. If you don't have a computer, the local public library does. If you have questions after studying a basic lesson, you can submit them and get answers. If you don't have anyone to take you, submit a request to be matched with a willing mentor, and you will be linked to an established mentoring group.

It will also be crucial to 'teach the teachers' especially if they have no experience.

Consider the case of a single mother who would love to take her kids fishing, but knows nothing about it. In short order, she can learn enough basics to feel confident leading her kids on outings. She is more likely to take them fishing, rather than hope they stop asking about it.

Consider the case of an experienced mentor who feels unqualified to lead outings in certain specific pursuits. Back to school he goes, where he quickly learns the essential basics of something new. That puts him back in the field, leading the charge.

Consider the case of an experienced bass angler who would like to try trout fishing with a fly rod. Back to school the angler goes, to learn something fun and new.

This can have an immediate and lasting impact.

It is called the School of Outdoor Sports.

You will find it at www.learnoutdoorsports.org.

About the Author

Mark Strand is an outdoor generalist raised in a family headed by his father, a passionate outdoorsman. He grew up fishing, hunting, and shooting for fun, changing the game as the seasons turned. Because he went fishing and hunting on some days he should have been in class, it took Mark five-plus years to be graduated from the University of Minnesota with a degree in Journalism and a minor in Fisheries & Wildlife. He has worked as a salesman in a hunting and fishing store, a manufacturer's representative in the outdoor industry, and has been a freelance outdoor writer, photographer, and filmmaker since 1977.

All of that has led to this, a passion to do something to help increase participation in his favorite sports. The remaining years of his career will be dedicated to helping newcomers become active anglers, hunters, and recreational shooters.

Strand lives in Minnesota with wife Jill, son Willie, daughter Samantha, a hunting dog named Ali, and an amazing collection of stuff needed to get outside and have fun.